Chyanne Myers was born and raised on a ranch just outside of Colorado Springs. She grew up as a middle child in a lower income family. At a very young age, she was told that she had a gift for writing and stuck with it throughout the entirety of her life. Chyanne suffers from PTSD and this has only given depth to her life and writing.

My baby boy, Josiah.

Chyanne Myers

BEAUTY AND THE DARK

AUSTIN MACAULEY PUBLISHERS™

LONDON • CAMBRIDGE • NEW YORK • SHARJAH

Ordering Information
Quantity sales: Special discounts are available on quantity purchases by corporations, associations, and others. For details, contact the publisher at the address below.

Publisher's Cataloging-in-Publication data
Myers, Chyanne
Beauty and the Dark

ISBN 9781645362388 (Paperback)
ISBN 9781645362395 (Hardback)
ISBN 9781645368588 (ePub e-book)

Library of Congress Control Number: 2022901436

www.austinmacauley.com/us

First Published 2022
Austin Macauley Publishers LLC
40 Wall Street, 33rd Floor, Suite 3302
New York, NY 10005
USA

mail-usa@austinmacauley.com
+1 (646) 5125767

Everyone who has impacted my life, and my love, for believing in me.

Final Song

I sit here thinking
The last time I wrote a poem
The last time I wrote a song
My last cry
My last hope
All I do is write one note
Tie a noose
Hang like a goose
I hate life
My last strife
Was with me and this knife
Cut me open
Cut me deep
I need to bleed
And pull my heart out
To see its final beat
Just to stop crying
I start biting
Piercing the skin
Hoping love will start again
Someone shoot me
Shoot me please
Save me from this fatal disease

But let me watch
Let me see
Put a mirror in front of me and leave
Let me watch me die
And watch death flash again in my eyes
Never had a chance
I never tried
So, I just watch and die
Live
Breathe
They're telling me screaming
They're saying it's not my time
Maybe they're right
One last fight
One last chance at life
But it's too late
I'm gone
And they'll keep listening to this
This is my final song.

I Can't Feel

I can't feel love
I can't feel hate
I can't feel the words in this poem I'm trying to make.

I can't feel happy
I can't feel sad
I can't feel the guilt when I do something bad.

I can't feel anything
I can't feel anything at all
But I can feel nothing every time I listen to our song

Pain

The pain reminds us
All that is beauty
All that is happy
And all that is love
Don't be afraid to feel something today.

Bleed

I scream in fear
Can you see my tears
My heart is pierced
And I bleed.

I scream
And bleed
This feels like a disease
I just wish I could leave.

There's too much blood
We're in a flood
There is no love
So, I'll still bleed.

Not Today Suicide

Soft shallow cries in the night
Love keeps me alive
As long as he's by my side
I have every reason not to die.

Emo's Poem

Forever afraid
Forever alone
My heart beats fast
But my soul is cold
At the end of the day
I sharpen my knife
Hoping to bleed out a better life
But the pain comes back
To haunt my head
Push people away
I'm alone again
Anger, fear and regret
They're my three best friends
But they disappear
At the bottom of my bottle
I'm alone again
Walk around with my head held low
To keep the reputation I built so long ago
But the sorrow has faded and now I'm just angry
Keep around the people I resent the most
I keep my distance and never get close
I am bound to be forever alone.

Envious

Everything you do is amazing
Everything I do
You do better
I'm envious of you.

Beauty
Talent
The boy
I'm envious of you
Envious of it all.

But I'm trying
Someday I'll succeed
Maybe one day
You could be envious of me.

Dead Bird

Dead bird
Dead bird
Lying on the ground
It took three weeks to decompose
Now your feathers are falling out.

Dead child
Dead child
Flying in the sky
Had to smack the birdy down
So you could be alone to cry.

Dead man
Dead man
Sinking through the floor
Had to kill the kid
'Cause your wife is such a whore.

A sad woman
A sad woman
She'll pick up the gun
Shoot herself twice
For what God has done.

A dead woman
A dead woman
She'll lie on the ground
She will never leave
And her spirit's still around.

Lonely girl
Lonely girl
Was put away for life
'Cause when the cops showed up
She was soaked in blood and holding a knife.

Roses Are Red

A rose
Draws blood
Conceals it in its petals
It absorbs the next soul
Love is just the color of blood.

Bleed
To love me
Bleed
To love him
Bleed
To break a heart
And bleed
Until you fall in love again.

In A World of Sin

The world is covered in darkness and smoke
But there is no flame
A world full of burning souls
But not one boil, blister, or burn
We are all damned
To feel a fire
That never shows
Covered in dirt
She removes her clothes
Taking off the sin
Just wash it down the drain
The flames still burn
Even more than before
She smiles and sins again
Accepting the darkness
She embraces the flame
She walks through the smoke
With a scared look on her face.

Nightmare At an Orphanage

An evil woman
With a crooked face
She lies through her teeth
She gets her way.

A pure child
With hopes and dreams
Sees through her act
He tries to leave.

A young girl
As cynical as she
Is his only hope
To break free.

The young girl
Devises a plan
Hits the woman on the head
And off they ran.

Through the meadows
They ran and flee
For a place where kids don't go missing.

Off to the side were two strange roads
One through the forest of haunting dreams
The other was a place of mystery.

To the place of mystery they went
The evil woman stood there in wait
Opened the door and said ham or beef?

He glimpsed in and they started running
There they were hanging by their feet
All the orphans that ever go missing.

The path of haunting dreams no one ever dared to go
Except for two young children
Whose story was never truly told.

Speak

She talks loudly
But never speaks
She runs away
And doesn't think
The consequences aren't fair
And are undeserving
She wants to be alone
But with everybody
She screams rape
But no one cares
She cries for hope
And no one's there
He strikes again
With a sly grin
She screams for help
And they're finally listening
Unsewn her lips
Now just the words are missing
Opened her mouth and her eyes
There she found a new meaning
She's moving on
By never moving on.

Without Words

24

A scar is a scar
Until someone gives it words
When you die, and scars remain
No words will be exchanged
Tell me how a body is so torn?
Yet still in place
A scar is a scar
Without someone to explain.

How To Define

25

She'll pick up the knife
Carve out letters in her skin
A gift god gave her
Would then become a curse
All it took was a few words
Now she hates herself
Scars define who she is
And the hardships she's endured.

Loving Wrong

A shimmer
A sparkle
But darkness lies
Behind her eyes
When he walks by.

Lifeless
A soul torn
Broken dreams
One hope for her remains
But he lives a different reality.

Embrace the darkness
Walk in the light
Hold his hand
And stay by his side.

Scream

A beautiful noise
It will be heard in the night
Nothing more calming and peaceful
Then someone begging for mercy.

Sharpening a knife
Then watch her cry
Watch her bleed
As tears stream out of her eyes.

Blood's so beautiful
Just one taste
It's the ultimate seducer
I cut her again to hear her scream
My body trembles with ecstasy.

Another and another
My body grows numb
I drift off to sleep
With the sound of screaming haunting my dreams.

A Royal in Red

Run, Run
Down the drain
Take it all
Leave nothing
Here I'll stay
Dripping
Scarlet pain
Hearts turn black
When remembering things
Turn cold
To not make new memories
It scars
Skin tears
Hearts are black
And I'm the queen.

Love For the Blade

A bite
A sting
A kiss
I thought I could resist
A beautiful thought
But it wasn't the same as last
The pain's no longer there
Now it's just a memory
But when I do it, that's all I need
Remember how that first kiss felt
Ashamed when I kissed him again
But the kiss was still great
To dance again
My tongue on your teeth
I crave it
Please don't deny me another
Forbidden
But our love is great
I can finally breathe
He kissed me again.

My Greatest Strength

I bleed
I boil
I blister
I burn.

I grovel
I plead
I disappoint
I run willingly.

No feeling is more complete
Nothing's made me so weak
Like ice melting in early spring
I have lost everything.

Faded
Life's one tragedy
As much as it kills me
It breathes more life into me.

I breathe powerfully
Every fail is a lesson learned
And every day I remember how to bleed